Pink Pussy Flower

a gift it's how he acts

Anastacia Burrell

pencil

ISBN 978-93-5610-714-4
© Anastacia Burrell 2022
Published in India 2022 by Pencil

Contributors:
Co-Author: Anastacia Burrell

A brand of
One Point Six Technologies Pvt. Ltd.
123, Building J2, Shram Seva Premises,
Wadala Truck Terminal, Wadala (E)
Mumbai 400037, Maharashtra, INDIA
E connect@thepencilapp.com
W www.thepencilapp.com

Author biography

I am a published author, writer, and storyteller. I love to tell stories for a living. I am an author, writing stories that come to mind. I may not be as infamous, but I am wondering if I will soon attract enough fans to show the world that I am the greatest author. I've always wanted to turn all my books into movies after they're written. Hopefully, I will see progress soon. Being an author is a huge inspiration, and I really enjoy the outcome of it. For me, a major production is a major. Storytelling is a blessing for me, so I will make my stories out of the best of my interests from the heart. Psalm 27:12 "The LORD is my light and my salvation, whom shall I fear? The LORD is the stronghold of my life, of whom shall I be afraid?"

CONTENTS

1. Pink Pussy Flower

Lil baby/rapper handsome In his song lyrics solid, Dominique Armani Jones, says, "Pretty pussy." But that is beside the point. I like Dominique Jones celeb. Yes, I like him, and I would like to meet Dominique in person. I have never met him yet, but I want to. But probably not. I'm just trying to get his attention to see what it's looking like. I really do like him. I want to see if my pretty pussy juicy to him because I want to fuck him once because Dominique is cute, so I want to feel how that comes back. I know it feels good to fuck Dominique Jones because I feel as if he is something special and sweet to me, and it's not about his money or anything like that. I was just wondering how those lips taste and hugs feel and if it's twerking like what he got there. Just kidding. No, this story isn't about Dominique Jones, but I'd like to give him this pussy gift to see how he acts up on me. No, I'm not a hoe or anything like that, or some kind of jump off quick pussy girl, or some type of sending niggas video hoe. I just want that feel-good thing come back. What's it like?

2. a gift it's how he acts

I just want to see if it's good and I want to see if Mr. Jones can make this pussy hot and wet for me. Let me see if it's real and hot. I'm ready to do MR. Jones in. I want to fuck you, MR. Jones. Sorry, MR. Jones. I am for real. I just want to make you moan. I've got that pussy gift for you, yea. I want to see if you can bend my legs over back to my head on the sofa or bed and fuck me real good in that front position. I want to see if it's good like candy. That's why I said Lil Baby Sweet and a special treat. YUM! Can I just feel those warm hugs and touch once? I bet Lil Baby hugs are good. I hope Lil Baby will contact me on social media. Come meet me there, boo. I see you, baby. On the other hand, let me change the subject from the celeb I liked to the nigga who has caused me so much hurt in my life. Do I need to say his name and who I'm talking about? Wait before anything goes on in the new testament of grace in the scriptures of Christ (Matthew 5:27-28). He heard it was said, Do not commit adultery, but I say to him that everyone who looks at a woman/wife in order to covet her has already committed

3. committed adultery

In his heart, he committed adultery with her. However, even though it is written in the Old Testament, verse 27, if you have heard that it was said by those of old saying, "Thou shalt not commit adultery." If a man sexually desires a woman, he has already committed adultery with her. In God's eyes, he shall not commit adultery. So let's continue with this situation alright. I'll start off by saying my pussy is so chocolatey and my pussy is so juicy, so once he comes over here to my home apartment at the back door, I unlock it for him to come on in. I know I have to take all my clothes off as soon as he gets here. Before and after bed, he took all his clothes off and laid down on my bed too. I got on top of him to ride him, and I went to kiss him on his lips. I could feel his kisses on my lips, and then after the intimacy, I got kisses during the intimacy. He was ready to go home whenever he was ready, I guess. Without having intimate knowledge, it feels so good to know that he loves me. After the fact, it feels so real. I felt good after that.

4. physical pussy power

He loves me up and down. It's so sweet. I can feel the sensation of a physical pussy power within me when he sticks it in and out of me. That happens when he is loving me the way I want him to love me because it comes into contact with my body senses of knowing my partner's intimacy and really feeling me. I can sense whatever he senses that contacts me. I feel my body deep down when he gets on top of me, sticking me inside and out. When he talks to me, I talk back. I feel a deep push down inside of me. I know that he wants me comfortably, it makes me feel like I am his girl. He is my boy. Everything he does brings peace to reality. When he bends my legs over and touches me with his strong two bare hands, I can feel the love between my pussy. My legs were hurting for a moment, but he had to put my legs down for a little bit, so I could get the pain out of my legs. My legs were still up, but it stopped just a little, quite slightly, so we could fuck right away. I feel so happy when he pushes his love inside of me, but when he first walks in to come see me, he tells me to unlock the door for him to come on in.

5. good pussy

he can't stay long. That's what he says. He can't stay long. I was like, "alright, ok, he doesn't want to stay long, but every since I have loved him." I've been single for a while now, no matter how hard I try, I can't seem to let him go. I will try to say no to fooling with him ever again. I tried letting him go once before. but it doesn't work. I seem to let him back into my life when things don't seem too right between me and him because he may get some other bitch pregnant. But he may always get she's pregnant and there's no telling when he might do it again. I just let him back into this good pussy of mine I have because it seems to me he can't get enough of me and it seems to me I can't get enough of him, so and so he is fine and so sweet. He is my baby and will always be my baby. He sweeps me off my feet when he steps into my back door of my room. I am his bae because he told me so. But sometimes he makes me mad when he does the wrong shit to me. I know my pussy will be good to him. And then he makes me

6. I cried

cry after the fact because he doesn't apologize because I believe he thinks he could do nothing wrong. I never told him why I cried. I keep my tears' business to myself. I never tell him when he comes creeping to come get my pussy because he will never listen to my heart about things I need to say to him. I always get ignored and some other bitch shows up in his life when it ain't right because of the crazy shit he does behind my back with other women. I hate it, for one thing, when he really does that there because it really pisses me off to the maximum extreme because I feel he's not doing right by me. And that's one thing I despise about him when it's based on some stupid nonsense I discovered about him years ago. I was supposed to be the good pussy in his life, not her. He wants to be with me at the end of the day, coming to see me to get some of this good ole pussy I have between my tights. The thing is, he shouldn't show any love to other women when he should be showing me that.

7. pussy power

I have the pussy power and love to start the show between us. I give it to him between my legs. I give him my brown-black pretty pink rose. Oh yes, he is such a bitch to me because he never wants to listen when I tell him to, but he goes the other way when I tell him not to. He wanders off when he doesn't need to. Yes, Paw, he's the whole problem in this book. I'll call him/he through this situation. Yes, but why doesn't he just listen to me for god's sake? I hope he straightens it out because I don't have time for his animosity crap. I am so tired of his bullshit. Sometimes I just scream from the top of my lungs because he just doesn't make any sense. He doesn't listen to me. Oh my gosh, he is just a muthafucka. But he wants to come get my pussy son of a bitch and push it inside of me whenever he gets the chance. I just can't imagine how he could do such things to me when he has a big wife crush on me, but I can't see myself in a marriage with him anyway. I will never settle for less than what I already have, putting my life at risk because this will never happen between me and him.

8. scumbag babes

I just couldn't see myself with him. It would have to be a small love relationship between me and him. It could never be a move into family life between us and him, because I don't want him like that. My pussy is far too beautiful to put up with his scumbag babes. My life is too good to be true to be fucking up my life with him, but it seems to me he has a lot going on for himself and is not looking forward to loving me the right way. I just don't see that in him. But though he wants to hate me for nothing and never wants to give me love and support, I can't think that he could ever be this way with me. How could he be so cruel the way he acted towards me when I gave him a gift of pussy power part of me? I let my guards down when I could just leave him alone. Because my life would be better off without him because he was the best thing in my life and could never be replaced. I just don't find other men very attracted just like him. It's been a very long time since we've been messing with each other. I don't have a baby with him. We just mess around a lot. Sometimes he just gets on my nerves. Sometimes on

9. fairy tale

things, he does half the time, but it never seems to go away. I try to think as positively as I can. When it does, it turns out horribly because I can't see how things are a fairy tale love between me and him, but when I think that I and him are a fairy tale, it always falls short of being as I expected it to be and it turns out to be too small for us not to live together to make peace with each other. All I can think of is just staying friends and having intimate time with each other each month. I would see him perfectly that way, and not sharing my life with him is exactly what I don't want. I just can't see myself having a family with him because I stay alone as a single woman. I would never want to rush into my love life. I would want to take it slow between me and him. I couldn't see myself rushing any faster than I was with him. I can see myself sleeping alone because with the person I'm sleeping with is a disaster. Sometimes I feel like not making a baby with him. I'm just not feeling it. He is really stuck in fuckout for sure, when things really piss me off,

10. fake facts

he takes me to play with Paw and doesn't take me seriously for anything. I can't stand the muhafucka. I'm going to keep calling him a muthafucka because that's what he is. I'm calling it on how I see it because there are some fake facts there and I won't take that shit back for anything. I can't even hide behind my ass about how I feel about him because there's too much shit going on today. I tell you, he is really something else. I'm at home every damn day and I'm not. I won't bother to think about his ass because I have no idea what he is doing behind my back, but he can cheat and do shit behind my back, but he's got another thing coming. I'm not worrying about the shit that he talks about because I'm going to live my life to the fullest. I'm not going to put up with any more trials in my life with him. I am not going to go through it with him. I'm not going to put up with him. I'm sorry. That makes it the other way around, this pussy. I've got bigger and better things to do with my life first. I put myself first, and there ain't nobody taking my space. I accept it as it is, the dick.

11. disobedient nigga

I don't have time for tests. I'd rather not have one. Being alone without him is not a challenge to being with him because I don't have to be with him or get married to him if he wants to be a disobedient nigga. Oh well, so be it. If he doesn't give a damn, then he has to accept his punishment. He can just move on to the left. I'm not having it with him because I'm not doing this with him anymore. I have a lot to attempt to achieve for myself, if he doesn't like it, he can kick rocks because he will never be a disappointment in my life because I don't have time to make moves in destruction in that order, so he doesn't want to get into my space because it is so tough and rough that he can't even see that what he has is good. He truly indeed messed up our friendship, but if that's the case, he wants to play that part, but as I said, I am not getting married and I'm not playing around either, I just want to be me. So if he ain't cool with that, that's his problem, but he's coming to get this big fat juicy pussy of mine anyway, I know it. I could

12. colossal asshole

never pointed out that this would continue on between me and him. I guess I like it though, but for a little while I don't, he becomes a colossal asshole. I see it never falls on him. I guess it never comes to a close with his situation with him wanting to always get my pussy and it's how he acts when he gets my pussy. He wants to share his body with other women. That doesn't mean a damn thing, but I embrace things much better than he could ever. Since he does the most out of everything, I'm getting something for him very soon. Let him keep acting the way he does because I'm not going to always be here when he needs me for intimacy. because I'm getting so tired of the disrespect and not getting enough credit for his crazy problems. What he did to me with his BM girls For a brief moment, I intended to do my thing because of him. But though, like I always said, though like I said, now back to the gift of my fat juicy pussy I have when he doesn't know how to act. When he gets it, he just makes things separate between me and him, but

13. stay a distance

when someone always comes in between us, we always stay a distance from each other. It never really seemed to work out between us because he wanted to do the opposite of his work, not wanting to be with me only. He has to do something else other than me, spend time with me, because that's what he wants to do. Do other shit and don't want to be with me. Take time out with us together after all. But he always has some BS going on. I believe, and I always believe, things are always something with him. He never wants to take things seriously with us, knowing what I'm saying. Do other things with me that are special, like going out to restaurants and having fun times with each other. But he wants to make things up by coming over to get my pussy, but that's not what I want him to come get my pussy. creating some type of intimacy. I don't have time for that. Life is not a game or a show to come across something so easy to get out of. This is not true that it is easy to put up with, it's hard and time is winding down.

14. backup alarm

And time is ticking and there's no space for mess for peace in my life because he is full of drama. and noises and brawls, but to remain silent and proud. I want to have it. I don't want some crazy show to pop up. start messing with what we share together is real, but I think it's too late to settle down with him. Because when it's time for a closer to settle with me and him, it's always a backup alarm that we can't be together. He always has something up his sleeve. He is always hiding. He always keeps his distance. Why keep a secret from me when I'm your twin flame? But though he doesn't act like a twin flame when he keeps cheating on me, why be so sickened by his sickening hoes? He's making other babies on me with these other hoes. These hoes are tired as hell. He should be tired of his hoes trying to come in front of him with shit every time he gets another bitch preg on me. But why, nigga? "Why nigga?" I asked because that's what I call him.

15. draw attention

The bitch is tired as fuck because he did nigga things to hurt me for the hell of it. That's what he is to me, a bitch as nigga because of what he does to draw attention to most things made of spikes for no reason. He brings nothing but problems. I'm in a drama with these jerks who want to hurt me. Instead of peace, he creates drama with me. He wants to make his horses bark for attention. He let shit come in between us. That's why he's not going to have anything in life with me. He makes things worse for me and him. When shit is brought to attention, the fuckup he causes, he backs up like a fucking pro. Star, the bitch, was going to say that the nigga was making babies on me, but in reality, the babies weren't made on me because he wasn't with me. He was with his bm fucking me to make other babies with me on his bm, so in other words, I was fucking with him the whole time.

16. deepest degree

They weren't together the whole time we were fucking. He was planning to get back with her. He was single, which is why we were seriously fucking. He just decided to put his hoe bm out in public for a change. So I don't know what she's talking about because afterward there were no babies on me, but there were babies made on his BM. He started messing around again afterward. I've never been last, so I'm neither the hoe nor the bitch. They are his BMS hoes and bitches. I'm most definitely not the horse. So really, I was able to be single. He went back to her. If I didn't care about him messing with her, I wouldn't be hurt. I really cared about him, so that really makes sense of why I had the right to feel the way I did feel about him. He hurt me to the deepest degree. It was just like a glass cut all the way through my skin. It really hurt me that badly. That should understand what that means if you've ever been cut with a glass.

17. king tuck

With these hoes, he acts like King Tuck, fooling with every chance he gets, sad and agg. His BMS is sad, but he wants to be with my pussy when he is ready for some I don't want his ass here coming to my home to get my pussy because I definitely don't need him for intimacy. I hate it when this nigga does things, I'm telling ya. This is for the dog. This nigga needs to get his self-esteem back because it ain't going to work. Between us, it ain't going to make it because a cheater will always be a cheater. I'm not begging or nigga to stay and support his ass. He's not using me for his children through new BMS and BMS. I've got to go without this nigga because I ain't having it. I thought about leaving his ass several times, but it never seemed to stop the intimacy between me and him. I'm not bothered by the fact that nigga was king tucking my pussy. But he thought he was thinking in his mind that it couldn't belong, he said to me when coming to get my pussy and to just think about me and him. We could never make it every month. People believe it's a

18. is a joke

game where me and him see each other. Every other month is a joke when it's not, but I could never put people in my business. because they always have something to say. I can never stand weakness in the face of a man. Never because I have too much pride and ego for that, and I couldn't see myself doing it. This kind of nonsense was done to me. I kept it real, 100%, but the thing is, he fell in love with me. But to really know the fact that it's true that he loves me, but why play a part in my life? Why should he come over to get it if he isn't paying for it? nigga I will always call him this because he ain't nothing but a nigga to me. But a piece of that, I see him coming over, trying to get some, which is all he wants from me, that's all that I am looking at right now. He's a piece of ass. But I could never feel too uncomfortable making love to him, and that's what he wanted. My dick always wants to make love to my pussy, but I get tired of riding him. I am so damn short-winded when I do, I want to get off of it. and let him do the rest. I can't go much longer than that. Then I think he's going to want me to keep riding him like there's no tomorrow.

19. I am riding

I can't stop wanting to stop. He wants me to keep going and flowing. I can't see myself keeping going when he wants me to keep going. I like it when he puts in work for me. I don't have to keep riding him for too long. I am not an energizer bunny, so I will just keep going and going. But he doesn't understand that riding too long makes a girl's legs get tired out. baby I can't go anymore. I am riding intimacy on him, but he sucks a mean tits out of me. I love it though, yummy. I like him because he makes my pussy go whoop whoop. I get some more lovin' in between my legs. Just slip that thing in me. I can't complain. I like it when he tells me to lie down on my back so he can get in the front. He just has to get some of this pussy cat of mine. He just comes out and makes my day, at least for a while. I have with him a piece of time, and his love can't keep me waiting for when he shows up at the back door to my room. I have a back door to my room, so how do we keep a secret when nobody knows he is in my room? It feels so good when nobody knows.

20. pops my pussy

He doesn't have to know anything about how I feel about anything when we do get together when he pops my pussy. Yay lawd, it's the moving of a movie play that he wants. He wants a video of me when he hits me from the back of my pussy cat. But let me get to that. He said I looked beautiful with the oil up on my ass. I knew I was gorgeous to him. I was a very attractive woman to him. Yes, I know I was. I enjoyed his words. I really did. I can't ever be enough for him. I am exactly what he wants out of love. I am his true lover. He wishes to be lovers and friends with me for the rest of his life. Yes, I must agree, but there are some exceptions. Changes need to be made to him in order for this relationship to move forward between us if he doesn't make any changes. It will never work between us, but it will never happen. I can see that now on here. Now I think he wants it badly, but what does he want from me? I've got nothing for him but all this

21. he's a boy

pussy that's pussy, that's it, and nothing can get past this pussy of mine because I don't have time to play with this nigga because all I can see is that he needs to get his shit together. Because there's nothing more left to do is be at home wondering what he's doing when he's not around me. I'm not sure what he's up to besides hanging out with his family and friends on Snapchat, but I know one thing: that's not all he's doing besides giving my thing away, my dick, yea. But he's a boy. He doesn't want to be a grown adult ass man, but he will never be a grown man because he hasn't made it to be an adult, but he wants to be a baby and doesn't want to be a grown man. I hope he grows up and finds out who he really is meant to be, but he probably will never be. I hope to see him become an adult instead of a little boy who does nothing meant to be small with us but not to come play with me and come get some of my pussy. I texted him one day and told him I was going to get him some pampers to buy for him, some baby bottles and nipples because he was a baby, and he was like ok. I was like, it would be cute when he was whipping his

22. sweet nuna

thing out, baby, he was like, "Really?" I was like, "Come on, give me a kiss and hold me. I bet I won't let go." YUP! I wanted to jump up laying on my back one day to kiss him and squeeze him, but I couldn't and I don't know why because something was holding me back. He was a sweet Nuna. I love the things he does to me when he comes to love me! He doesn't really need pampers, bottles, nipples, or anything like that. He just needs to grow up and be a husband to me, which God knows isn't going to happen for me, or he just needs to be an adult for me to provide something for me. He doesn't have to be a husband to me but do something for me, which is like begging for something to happen for me. He isn't going to listen to me anyway about the situation, but he knows how to get some pussy from me when he wants it. If he knows how to do that, he should provide for me. He never listens to me. He listens to himself, but it is very strange that he doesn't want to listen to me or to what I have to bring to the table.

23. grow up

I can't see myself raising a little boy when I have a son of my own and I don't need another adult son to come into my life to beg me for help. Like the man I'm not raising is an adult I'm having an affair with, I have to support him when he can help himself. He is grown and doing what he needs to do to best take care of himself. He is in his twenties, later he will be in his thirties. I don't need a boy to follow me around for help and support because somebody is already growing here with me and needs my help. My son I have to support. I ain't about to take care of a grown-ass adult when I have my own baby to raise to see my big boy grow up. I'm raising my big boy solely. I was pregnant for nine months, based on the fact that he was getting someone else pregnant by being childish with these hoes. I had a seven-year relationship with paw. On the other hand, I knew I had to raise my son. I don't need to raise another little boy to be a mommy when I'm already a mommy to one boy, who is my son. When I had him, I had to see him grow up as a child, all the way up to a teen. And I still have a lot more to see my son grow up to become a man. Giving a gift is when I give it to him, he starts to act up like

24. advantage

he can't do right by me when the rule is told to when he doesn't do it and he tries to take advantage of it on what I already told him once. He takes it and runs with it, doing what I told him to do. He didn't do it. I live my life by the rules: if he isn't taking care of me, I'm not meeting him anyhow. No other way. I keep my distance, stretching so far away from him that I'm not attempting to make another move or step with him. I'm out to stay single forever. I don't have time for it because he is always looking to have other girls because he is a young man and could be looking for another girl in his twenties or he could be looking for another girl when he is much older than he is now. I ain't having it. I deserve better because he doesn't deserve me at all. He needs to go. It's not meant to be so selfish in this relationship we have together, because it's not meant to be so selfish in this relationship. But I will never see him anyway. When he's ready to come over, he's coming to my back door. But he's been coming to my back door room for a long time, every since I moved across town, but

25. backroom door

the other home I was living in, he was coming from the front to the back door. But where I'm staying at now, he likes to come to my backroom door, which he never goes to. People and his family and friends are trying to make it seem as if he is calling me to get on me about some shit, so he has to call me to get me straight. If he calls me to get me straight, ain't no nigga going to call me and get me straight, I corrected him. That's when things got dicey with the cuckoo girl bm thinks she knows it all and everything, but she doesn't. She's just upset because I'll be making love to her BD every month when he comes to get some of this pussy cat of mine. That's why she's a mad ass. Because if it was meant to be, it would be and what would have happened for us to be together? She would have been more mad. But enough said. He ain't paying for my pussy, so why be with him? I'm not sure what that means. Why is he so worked up for no reason? Why should I be stuck on stupid bs when everything is bs to me? because I stay home by myself. I don't need him to be around

26. remain friends

me because I don't need him for anything and I don't have anything to lose and nothing to gain from his trust, which I don't need from him and I most definitely don't need his trust because that's been over with between us, so he been lost that long time ago. I was through way back then, so I'm through right now in the present time. So what we can do is stay and remain friends, as we did once before. As always said, this pattern is always going to repeat itself. So let us embark on this journey so that our friendship can last. If we continue on, the challenge will arrive now because we are never getting married if this test must go on between me and him. This will never be a relationship seeing us as a family together, but he always comes back to me to get this pussy of mine when he wants it, I always let him back into my life for intimacy, but I am all for myself and don't need any help or support from him. I'm going to keep working for what I want, I'm going to keep grinding even if a nigga doesn't work for me. I make my own bread. I create my own hustle and the motivation for what I do.

27. support myself

said that I don't need him for support because he does some fuckup shit when he wants to do it behind my back, but he is looking for support from me and I bet he ain't getting it, so he might want to get it from his stupid bms because I ain't his bm. I'm looking to support myself only. I'm not worrying about anyone else but me. I'm just looking forward to the game of my future. I can bring it to myself and nobody else but myself. I can understand. He asked what I was doing. I said hey, I was sleeping, and he was like oh and I was like oh what? I was mixed in my sleep, so I was trying to get it right when I was texting him back for some love, so I couldn't get anything right but to just get out of bed. I was just getting up, I didn't know he texted me in the morning. I was laying down trying to get up. I didn't text him right away. I just didn't feel like I was texting him right, so I told him was he still coming? I was still feeling bad for some reason. A little bit. I mean, I was sleeping when he texted me this morning. I mean, sorry

28. he caught me

for the spelling and grammar, my boo. He caught me off guard this morning. That's how I was feeling! I hope he comes later! I need his good love! And he was like, "Who is there?" I was like, "Meee, is he coming tonight and what was he doing?" He was chilling and asking what I was doing. I was in bed all day, lol. He was like, "Still feeling bad?" I said, "Wait, let me check, yea, I am." He was like "damn" and I was like "damn what?" Why was he worried about coming over now? Just give me that boy, whatever you've got. I asked the nigga how many children he has now, but he never responded. Oh, paw selfish jerk. But he knows how to tell me about another woman's picture he had sent to me in a text message. I can't even tell how many children he has now because he had another baby on me with another girl. But I ain't having it bruh. He is so in the wrong. He needs to kick rocks. And get the fuck out of my face for real, because we no longer have any meaning. There's no meaning to the situation anymore. That's over with. I just can't see us being

29. satisfaction

together after the fact that he did this to me, I just feel like he's a hoe and will never change for the better. There will never be an understanding between us. I will never give him a satisfaction guarantee. No, indeed, I want, but he thinks he has it made with me. This relationship we had will never be enough for us to get married. As I previously stated, again and again, that's been dead for a long time, so far. and will never, I believe, ever return to any kind of committee. because he ain't husband material. He will never understand how it feels to be a pussy and not a dick, like him as a dickhead. And I'm not supposed to understand how he feels about his situation because he acts like he doesn't care. So if he doesn't care, I don't care either, so he may want to go deep into that water by himself because I ain't going deep into that water with him. I did whatever with him. and ain't going for it. It doesn't matter anymore to me. I'm not doing this, "no no no." I've been hurt by him twice in the role, but not just twice, three times. He has been playing too many parts on

30. latex condoms

me and I just can't deal with the shit anymore and I'm not putting up with his shit anymore. I am a lady of power pussy that can't be discriminated against and it's something he has to deal with in the future, not me. It's not my problem, it's his problem. I'm not giving in to anything he does to me at all. Whatever he thinks he can do to me, I ain't falling for it either and I don't care. I texted him about giving me some of that yum yum making love and he said when? I said, "Whenever, that's how we thought." I sent him some condoms with a picture of a condom full of condoms. It was about the counting of fifteen condoms in one picture I took and sent to him. I got green condoms and they were called Fantasy Brand Latex Condoms with purple, blue, green, yellow, and red colors written on the front of the Fantasy Condoms. I told him I got these condoms from my doctor's office and I told him he could not have them. It's only for me and him to come play with my pussy while I get him hot and he was like ok and I was like ok that baby said ok awww but I know his ass ain't no awww playing with my

31. texting me

pussy but he likes me, though I know he does. I am always getting angry at him because he plays with my emotions too much because he plays too damn much, and I don't have time for games, and I am not playing with him. I am so serious right now that I can just knock him on his ass because he's got another new bitch preg on me. Naw, what's up? I spread myself away from his ass. Because he keeps messing up shit, nigga has gone completely insane. I despise seeing this nigga struggling because I'm not going to be there for him when he needs me. But I get it. He's going to be mad and mad, yea and he will be mad, but I don't care. This nigga is texting me for some pussy, but I give it to him anyway, though but he ain't worth my time of the day. I ain't playing with him, but that's how love goes and that's how the story goes. I just can't see myself with this nigga from time to time in public. No way, hosay, he will never fit my protege, and my protege is way too fire boo and I don't give a two fuck. It's always how he acts all the time, and I know he is coming back to get some of

32. dummy things

This cake is a dessert muffin. He is going to be all up in me. Do I enjoy humm? My guess is as good as mine. So really, he just never makes one point with his dummy things. He will never be what he says. He will be with me again. And he should not try to make out for anything because he can leave that where it's at. But at some point, he's going to want to be with me, and I'm not going to go for his games. I'm at home chilling waiting for him to send me a text message to tell me he's coming over to get a piece of my pie. But he isn't right, and he knows he isn't right, but he'd better not think about anything but trying to use me for his efforts, and I ain't no ATM machine. and that's what I'm not going to be to him. He better go get it from his girls and not me. because the ball role isn't here, but I got his ball role full of games he wants to play with me. and I'ma show him how to play the ball role because I ain't his battlefield full of games. He takes me to play with, and I'm not his average play toy. I'm not the one to be fooled into playing games with him. because he thinks it's a game

33. messed-up self

when I tell him I'm not going to mess with him anymore, he's like OK. I'm going to give him the green light. OK, Paw Butthead, I was not playing with him when I told him I was not going to mess with him anymore. However, he was a jerk in the beanstalk head nigga. He thinks his drama is sweet to me, but it's not. He's been in way too much trouble lately for me. I haven't heard from him in minutes. I know he's all about himself, like always messing with me on Snapchat and other bitches behind my back. I said once before, like always, he is too busy messing with me. He plays too much. I'm not sure about his messed-up self, but I haven't been thinking about him lately. I will never ever be able to say all kinds of things about this little boy. but I just don't care when he then messes me over. I don't care anymore about him because I don't want to cuss him too much. But I'm cussing for a reason, because cussing ain't good for cursing like a sailor. I know, why? Because when he disrespects me, I can't tolerate it anymore. It's too much to handle after that. I had about enough of his

34. foul-mouthed

ass, so much that it makes me call him all kinds of names out of the book. I swear to God, this nigga will be cursed. I really have a foul-mouthed. I'm feeling this way because he then hurt me twice. I only think of him for intimacy. I think about not being with him. do I think about being his wife? "No." As a result, I'm not interested in being his wife. He better not propose because I'm not feeling it because I'm single and I'm not having it because I'm straight and loving myself to the bone. from Louisiana. I live in it and ain't looking for anybody to hold me down. That mess on top of me and all that cuddling to forcefully suffocate me I don't need that because I'm free in the universe and nobody can touch me. I can do what I want and when I want. I can do bad and good by myself. To finish this with the love life I had, it went from worse to sour. I am lost in broken love. My love life started off very slowly and very smoothly. He was so handsome and sleek, I never thought in a lifetime I would ever find someone to have an affair with, to love on me every month. He will come see me once a month. I just can't imagine how he did It.

35. first glance

I remember what month I first met him. I saw how his eyes fell on me with love. At first glance, I knew it was genuine. I couldn't believe it was genuine love. I finally found my twin flame. I imagined that this would last forever. I believe this is love because I know it is. When I feel something, I know it's real love. I know it's love and there's never any turning back to someone else. If it wasn't meant for us to be together, it wouldn't have been when we first met. I knew he was my first love. because nobody could ever tell me anything different about him. I have seemed to be attracted to his sensibility, which really draws me to him the most. because every time I see him, I feel at ease and intimate with him. I could never imagine how wonderful it could be for me and him to have the love of our lives. And when I saw him before, we hadn't come close to each other just yet in the club. When I first saw him in there, we hadn't gotten a chance to talk to each other right away. I did see him at "Joe's Lounge", and Joe's was one deep that night

36. meet-up

and a lot of fun! But, when I got really close to him, I got in the car and took a seat in the back seat of his cousin's car. Although we weren't having a conversation at the time, he was really close to me in the back seat. He was to my right and I was to his left seat at the back of the car. Mostly, he was sitting by the door to the right because we were all coming from "Joe's Lounge" to take him home. I was feeling like I liked him. I never responded to him in the car at the time because I was so busy and too busy wanting his cousin to take me home because it was dark that night outside the club and we both didn't respond back to each other while sitting in the back of the seat next to each other. That was way back in "2015" when we first met. It was a meet-up again on social media (Facebook), and he came to my home, and it was a meet-up together that night with text messages back and forward to meet up to see each other for the first time. We walked outside together, about to go into my home to unlock my door with my key ready to go

37. love story

in that night, we made love for the first time. We had an affair, making out in my bed. We've been messing around for "7 years" and it has to go on for "10 years" and more, and I know he loves me because he had plans to marry me. But things aren't going right for us or making progress as slowly as they should be. But between me and him, me being a free-will single lady, And as for him being a single boy, he does not want to grow up. He's "28 years old" and we have been making love nonstop for months. But he wants to be with other women and doesn't want to support me, so I don't have time. So I guess this marriage thing is not going to happen for us since he wants to say "block" to our relationship, because I don't know what that means when he says "block." If this is a love story, this is how we are. All of us women will want to know why it is so hard to be romantic. Why do we have to take it slow? I guess not. It's not called "taking it slow." It's called seeing other people until we decide to be together. No,

38. submission acknowledgment

don't agree with this love life we have with each other. "Nooo way." We are not taking it slow because he wants to do what he wants to do behind my back, be with other girls and not listen to anything I have to say to him. But I believe, romantically, he has to provide for me first and not make me prove it to him. I don't want to be the provider because I'm the lady and he should take a stand by bowing with regard to me kneeling down on one knee and body in submission acknowledgment. But if he doesn't, then well, there is no relationship between us if he doesn't show me that I am long gone, out of his life forever. I ain't never coming back. I don't have time for black thug love. I want white love and respect because I truly believe white love shows black women like me love and support with respect. I found out the truth about his wanting to be with someone else and not me. I believe I was the special one in his life for him, which is I'm someone he has a connection with. I don't want to be with someone that causes me so much suffering in my life and

39. base-side chick

Why? Because I'd rather take a step back and be a single lady than put up with his nonsense with other girls I don't have time for. I'd rather be alone, of course, instead of seeing him with someone else at a restaurant table eating beans and lemon martini cocktails, drinking a wide tall glass with another base-side chick. So what is it for me to be left alone? I hate the fact that I have to go through so much with him to try and leave him alone, but what good is it for me to be left alone? I guess a lack of understanding between me and him means he will never understand me, so he is always MIA. It's not easy to leave someone that I have been soul tied to for too long and I just can't let go. I feel as if he is not my soul tie, so what is it when I give him my pussy that makes things right for us? Nothing right. It's always going to be the same for me and him because he will never change, but he wants more on some other level new between us, but he ain't making that move between us. When it's going to happen because he

40. soul tie shit

never make the right decisions for us. Why think of something new for us and don't do it? Why talk about it and don't do it? But he wants something. I don't want what he wants, which is not right for us. I don't want that because he didn't listen to me about what was right for us, so what can I do after that? soul tie, Ya right. I would like to see more of this soul tie shit. So me and him can get going on because I can't stand this shit with him. I'm not going to take any of his bullshit that he put me through by giving other hoes money. Not me, but that's a damn shame for him to be treating me wrong in this way. How could he be my soul mate when he had other bitches and hoes on me? I am sick of it and it is time to make a change to his negative attitude and selfish ways. I know for one thing, he will never change for the better. I'm sure he's insane. He's just so strange and cuckoo. He is dumb at times to not know he has something good in his life, which is me. I retaliated so harshly against him because he treated me so poorly. which makes me want to be with someone else

41. niggas videos

And trust me, I am not a cheater. I only do this because he likes to fuck other girls. He wants to tell me over text messages that I'm sending niggas videos when he's the nigga I've been sending videos to. Why does he say such crazy things to me when all I've been doing is with him over the years? It's been a very long time since we've known each other and he wants to say such crazy things to me like this because if he feels as if I've been sending niggas videos, I just want to go be with one nigga. If he's going to think this way about me sending niggas videos, in other words, I don't send other niggas videos. I've got too much class for that to be doing that, but he's out cha with some other girls, getting ready to make a future with them, being a hoe and not wanting to be with me, but he wants to give me a wet as to show my pussy off to him for no reason. I don't have time for the pity games he plays around with me for no reason. I don't have time because if that's what he wants to do is play well, then I'll let him continue on playing games because the game is going to be played my way

42. kiss my ass

I'm going to show the world that I'm better. Anyone who doesn't know me is welcome to kiss my ass. I'm not here to kiss anybody's ass to get alone with them. To make the situation clear, I am a tough girl cookie when it comes down to matters, functions, rights and wrongs, so I could never go wrong in a matter of time. I see deep before I leap into things. When things don't seem right for me, I try to let them go and rebuke them because I know they aren't true, so I'm down to make whatever happens to me happen because I'm the queen boss too. Whatever happens, I'll take it. I am strong enough to handle things the right way for me and not worry about what he or she says about my relationship with a man. Yes, it's all good because I have trained myself to just take whatever challenge comes my way as easily as 1, 2, 3, and flow with it. I go with the flow with it and live my life and never delete it because it's worth the fight to keep something in mind to show the world off for and to keep it as a project and steady paste and learn

43. A nigga

It would make my life much easier because it can withstand a quick use because those with a good heart don't mind it. If interested, then he or she is not interested in me, but come on now. It isn't true, but he is just not into me. There is no such thing. He is not interested in me. And he could never turn this pussy down for anything. I would never be a retard, ritardo, or retarded lady to do anything in order to make myself look bad in front of others. I'm too confident for a nigga to take me out of character and take me out on my flippers and socks to use me to get what he wants out of my pocket to drain me of my money. I don't think so. He's never done anything for me over the years. Of the affair I had with him over the years that have passed by. I'd rather be happy alone and stay alone for eternity. He even tried to ruin my life by trying to bring girls into my home. I don't want a nigga to come into my life, causing me problems with what he is doing wrong. I don't understand what makes him able to run my life to

44. cookie

bring girls around me that aren't women. Sometimes I wonder why he causes so much upheaval because, at the end of the day, I just want an affair and nothing more or nothing too serious or less to happen for us to get too close to each other. I'd rather stay away from him and the people he hangs around with. I don't want to get close to him and I don't want to be there with anybody he knows, making me get close to this nigga and the people he's around. But enough of this chaos. He's always wanting to be the first to jump into my cookie when it's time for my goodies, but he's always ready for that and nothing really matters. The only thing that is important to him is intimacy, so he goes home. This other person that's not in my life, he's not interested. Why is he not interested? If I feel as if he is not interested in me, I would feel as if he is not interested in me either, so it is dumb and stupid to know someone has told me he is not interested in me, which is not true. I would never ask a man out on a date with me if I thought I felt negative toward him. who I thought was positive. I felt he was a good person. But this isn't the man I'm referring to

45. another sister

I want him to come by and get my pussy from me, to unlock my door and come on in to get some. The years have flown by my soul tie. Nope, that's not who I'm talking about. I'm talking about another person. It's someone else. It's not the man I've been having an affair with for a very long time. It was another man. Some little girls are really sad that they look like grown women when they are not. I have never seen a grown woman put another sister down like me to say such lies about me or have a funny negative feeling about a man I like who has a huge crush on me. She is going to say that he doesn't seem to be as interested in me as I am in him. Also, the chances of me having a sexual connection with him look really bleak. I could try and talk to him if I like, but it doesn't seem to be a possibility. I must keep my expectations low here, she said to me. I feel as if I don't have to do shit about keeping my expectations low. Oh wow, how childish of a woman of her to bring me down, but she ain't no woman telling me childish, foolish, stupid, crazy dumb messages on how

46. time we fucked

this is disturbing. It can be frustrating. There is no trying to talk to him or any way to keep any expectations low. It's not low between me and him, and there's no bleakness in our intimacy. I don't think so. But anyway, my soul tie needs to keep it real, so how does he want me to keep it real? When my soul tie isn't trying to keep it real with me, I see this is a game for him that he wants to keep seeing me for intimacy. But that shouldn't happen. Why? I can't believe how many affairs I have had for over seven years. It has failed a lot of times. My relationship with him ended in disaster, but I remember when I first met him, it was peaches and cream a little bit. Because of the sex, the first time we made love, it felt like blind sex at first sight. I didn't know about this nigga burden of suffering. What he was about to do to me in the future was going to be so cold-hearted that he fucked over and hurt me for that girl. His past was very different from the time we fucked. He had short dreadlocks on his head before they grew much longer down to his back. His dread grew over the years, very much longer now

47. I'm single forever

since we had been having an affair over the years, it was alright. The affair was alright, but there was so much drama with so many girls he had put first before me, which was really sad. I didn't like it at all. He really did hurt me a lot, but though I'm glad I'm single forever. I'm going to stay that way, but with me right now, it's all about sex and no relationship. I'm just not feeling it anymore because I have been treated wrongly many times over the years by him. It's been krama with this nigga over the years and I ain't having it. As I said, it ain't right. It's been that long since I've been giving my pussy away to him for years and he hasn't really appreciated it or given me the chance to love him the right way. He just passed me on up for girls like I wasn't shit to him. What could I do for him when he keeps on putting other girls first before me? I can't be there for him if he ever goes to jail. I'm not going to be there to hold him down. I will hold him down when he needs me to give him this cat. I am not his battery charger. When it's time to make a comeback, when he needs me, though it's like a mystery, crying

48. he wanders off

oversplit milk when this game is not worth my time, as well as dignity, pride, esteem, and character, When in place, he wanders off. Don't come back to me only to sex me once a month. It was too much and I couldn't take it anymore, but though I'm happy to be free from this nigga, that doesn't mean anything to me. I'm cool though, just being by myself and waking up on the side of my bed alone by myself. Instead of being with a nigga that gives me headaches, I feel so much better. Being without him just made my day much better today. Without him, there is a sense of liberation. I must go on to a better life and a better mood, but watch me grow. I will grow without him because I don't need him in my life, which is better off. I must admit that I live my life to the fullest until I reach bliss. From where I live, I pay to be the boss. I enjoy it. I lived it until death did me apart because I couldn't be apart from myself. I could never be broken in the dark by a nigga that didn't want the good to keep a woman like me with him. I was going to treat him right, but he kept on going to other bitches on

49. dogging me out

me behind my back. I ain't fucking with him like that, so I'ma get this shit out of the mud. He keeps on dogging me out, so what else? What am I supposed to do next when he keeps bringing other hoes out on dates to restaurants when I am at home laying down with nothing to do but chill? I was in my room thinking about nothing to do. I'm not going to say anything about what he does. He just keeps leaving me for other bitches. But I don't want him to think that way anymore. Imma just laid down the table for us. He goes his own way, and I'm going my own way because the only thing left to do is move on. I want to move forward to a healthier life for myself and not for us to make a future together. No, I don't want that. I don't want to be with him like that. I guess the affair is just better off until then and afterward until something happens to me. And then what's going to happen after that, I don't know, because I'm not looking for Romans. Nope, I just want to be left alone without being unhappy with him. I can say this one more time. I can't stand to be with a person like him. I just can't stand to be what

50. friendship partner

really happens for us to be together later in life because I don't want to be with him anymore. I thought sex was going to take control of our lives and stay as a friendship partner together forever, which is what he wanted it to be. But though this didn't happen for us, which is eternal, he wants to call me private to get back together, but I ain't having it because I'ma tell why I ain't having it because I'ma laydown everything real soon and why. Some more spilled milk on the table, some more gossip about this situation. Why does he call and cuss me out, asking me why I fucking blocked him on Snapchat like I wanted to fuck with him? Why should he call and play to see if I want to fuck with him because I don't have time? He always has to do things when we are deciding. He texts me instead of calling me. He normally doesn't call, but he ends up calling me with a private number just because he wants to come back into my life. because he normally texts me instead of calling me. I ain't having it this time either. I hung up on his ass this time when he went to go cuss me out and I said

51. blocked him

What? He said, "I fucking blocked him and I hung up on his ass." YUP, I sure did, because I clearly found out why this relationship between us was so bad. My life between me and him ain't going to stick forward. I'm not going for his drama not today. I don't know, I made myself this promise. I will heal myself from this hurt and sadness he has caused me for real. He has caused stupid shit and I will never want to be hurt like this ever again in my life. I fucked with him, messing up my life. He was crazy, but I found myself with an open wound. Staying with him doesn't make any sense. I'm not trying to run back into it with him like this ever again because I was trying to make things right between us. He isn't timeless to finish the friendship we had with each other. I needed to put my legs and feets down in this situation with him and say no so I could heal and move on forward with my life without him. I don't need to spend the rest of my life with him. I don't want to spend the rest of my life with him.

52. sexual relationship

I don't get along with him at all. Why spend it with him when I can spend it with another man like Armani? I wish I could spend it with Dominique Armani Jones. I do not want to spend it on a lover who I have been dealing with for over seven years. It's not worth it if I'm sexually and emotionally attached. It's not my time to sit around wondering when he's going to when I can spend it on somebody that is worth it, like Dominique. I don't want to lose myself being who I am today because I deserve better and I deserve a better friend indeed. I never felt physically in a sexual relationship. I didn't like that we were emotional instead of physical. It was like, with us together, hey, he's going to take care of me physically. It wouldn't be like that at all in our friendship. It would always be a constantly repetitive emotional attachment with us in intimacy all the time. There would be no play or action. It would never be one hundred percent with him with us together. It would always be about him and his needs with other women. He would put himself first and not me. He was very

53. playing mind games

selfish and still very negative towards me. He prioritizes himself. I'm still not first to him, which is really sad, and he would be the one to hurt me emotionally. Relationships are always an issue. I hated that he did this to me. It will always repeat itself every fucking time with him constantly. It will always hurt me deep down inside. I could never understand why he would hurt me emotionally like this. I'd cry in my room because he'd have someone else in his life in front of me. I know I'm worth more. I would never waste my time helping a man get through anything when he is not a man. When he wants to be childish, digging in my pussy and playing mind games with me, he is a man to me. I don't need him if he's going to cheat on me with other girls. I don't need a man who isn't going to pay attention to me. I couldn't see myself or imagine myself with him doing great things together because I feel as though he doesn't appreciate it.

54. never a TV fanatic

I'd like to tell everyone how I first became interested in Lil Baby, so when Dominique Armani Jones read this news about me, I was intrigued. I want Dominique to be amazed at how gorgeous he is too. I want to get to know Dominique, the one and only heart, my man. Dominique Jones I saw Lil Baby on the big screen on television because he has always been beautiful to me, but it wasn't the pub until I saw Lil Baby. I was never a TV fanatic or a Google research fanatic. Having no cable or laptop wasn't a problem for me. Sometimes I had to struggle to get to where I was. I needed to rest my head, but the struggle was good. Amen to the heavenly father up above. The clouds are white and the skies are blue. I am religious. I love the Lord, but I really didn't know Lil Baby was out there like that in public until I did some research in 2020 before the year was almost over. I saw Lil Baby had a girlfriend, but I didn't know who Lil Baby was and who his

55. perfect timing

girlfriend was who he was with. As I said, I had to do some research on this because I really didn't know Dominique Jones at all when Lil Baby first started out on the big screen. What Lil Baby did when Dominique was 21 years of age and first started in the rap industry and what Lil Baby said, Lil Baby said in one of his rap rhymes, "Perfect Timing," after Lil Baby got out of prison for two years at age 19. "Lil Baby" said, "Perfect timing." On one of Lil Baby's albums, it was this song, My Turn. Back in 2020, "Humble" was released as one of my favorite songs on the Lil Baby album. I was like, "Lil Baby started when he was 21 in 2017, huh right?" not sure. However, I believe that Lil Baby began much earlier. If he released new albums in the coming years, he couldn't be 19 years old, right? It was 21 yea, when Lil Baby first started. That was one of my favorite songs on one of Lil Baby albums, "Humble" and "My Turn." I had no idea, but that tells me a lot about how busy I was during those days. Many years passed without knowing that this young, beautiful, rap star, Lil Baby, was out there doing his thing.

56. finest rap star

It was at the end of 2020 that I really began to get to know Lil Baby better. through 2021 I didn't know Lil Baby started in 2017 by signing a record deal with Atlanta, Georgia. In the U.S, 4 Pockets Full (initialized 4PF) was an American record label back in 2017. I never knew. Artists like Lil Baby, who is such a beautiful rapper, could be the best and finest rap star in the game. Of all the male rappers, Lil Baby was the one that caught my attention. "Oh baby, Lil Baby" was. fine ass hell, my man, Lil Baby, but I've been so busy that I didn't notice him on the big screen. I'm sure everyone is wondering how I didn't notice that Lil Baby was famous like that. I had a family with television, but 'heyyy' I didn't realize it wasn't my fault and the Lil baby was out there big. I saw the baby was made of butter and chocolate cream. sexy gentleman when I had really found out about Lil Baby's fame and riches, that was when I was really starting to get to know Lil Baby better when I did my research at the middle of the end of the year

57. straightforward

finally, I saw all those pictures with those images of Lil Baby and his girlfriend together, but I still didn't know they were out there hot and heavy in public like that. When I did find out, I looked up the research history of Lil Baby and Girlfriend because I wanted Lil Baby to be my boyfriend. I am straightforward. If I was to ever meet Lil Baby, I wanted to get to know him in the future. I'm doing some research on Lil Baby, my man. I was thinking, "I wish I had known about this Lil Baby before Jacquees and I were flirting on Facebook Messenger, but I had never met Jacquees." But I never got to see him in person because I was never the traveling and vacationing, concert-going type. I was always in the house. Whenever I needed to go somewhere, I would walk or call for a cab. I paid $10 for a taxi cab to take me here and there, back and forth to the store. And back home, it would be around my hometown in Franklin, Louisiana to Super 1 Foods, I would shop at Walmart in Franklin, Louisiana, my hometown, even though I was on food stamps

58. empty basket

I couldn't complain about how much food I'd have to buy. I was on my food stamps because it was enough. It was enough to take care of my two. My teenage children at home. Walking from my home address to Franklin supermarket was a short walk for me to make my grocery list for me and my two teenage children. I'll walk. I carried my empty basket to the store, to Franklin Supermart, because it would be too far for me to walk. Pushing my empty basket from home to the grocery store would be close for me to walk to the store. I would come back home with a bag full of groceries in my basket, walking on the sidewalk all the way home, pushing my basket all the way home with my hands and legs and shoes. I was just walking, struggling with my basket, sincerely trying to get home. However, I would normally walk from here to there to get to where I needed to go

59. goodies

sometimes I will walk all the way to the store and push my grocery basket to get some groceries and come back home to my two teenage children to eat all the food I made at home, like all the goodies, cake pies, cookies, candies, hot packets, all different kinds of frozen pizzas, cane goods, 4 salads in a plastic container, 4 gallons of low-fat milk, 6 boxes of honeycombs, tricks for kids, raisin brands, lucky charms, cinnamon toast crunch, Brown Cocoa Puffs cereals, 5 gallons of Sunny Delight to drink, and two gallons of Hawaiian Punch. The rice is in the plastic bag, red and white beans and sausages are in the box. One gallon of yogurt, ham, cheese, and bread. grits in the box. 2 packs of bacon and frozen breakfast sausages. Pancakes in the box, a pack of frozen chickens, chicken wings, and waffles are my favorite meals. I love to make fried chicken wings and waffles or pancakes with chicken, some honey, and hot sauce on top, Louisiana style. I love to cook country food my way because

60. I'll cook soon

My two teenage are always hungry and want something to eat. I'll cook soon. When I get home from making my packages, I will have five frozen packs of meat and many more. I finally make it home and unlock my front door with the one key I have around my neck. I made a shoestring necklace to wear around my neck, which I'll tuck inside my shirt. I don't like it on the outside of my breast where my titties sit with my shirt on. Sometimes I'd use my other second key, which is the same as the one on my zip tie key. I'll tie that and I'll put it somewhere in my pocket or I'll put the key in my bookbag purse when I start to walk to get my groceries. When I finally get home, I finally get my door to open with my one key. I slowly enter my house, carrying several grocery bags in my arms. I pushed the basket into my home full of packages to take out packages and put them in my monthly refrigerator. I push my basket full of groceries into my living room or kitchen where food and groceries have to go

61. Dragon Ball Legends

in my refrigerator and cabinets. On the top of the cabinets, it says what I pay for every once a month with my fixed income. I also get government assistance from the state to pay off $111 a month at affordable home furnishing bills and I keep my refrigerator bill for affordable home furnishing bills paid every month. When my check would come in every 1st and 3rd of the month, the basket would stay in my home until I was done taking out all my groceries and I would see my teenage son in my living room playing XBOX games such as Dragon Ball Legends. There are many more legendary Xbox games, like Mortal Kombat, but I will always see that my son will be more into Dragon Ball Legends than the other games. He has a bunch of games on his Xbox. I could name them all, but my son favorites are Dragon Ball Legends. Those would be the games I see my son playing all the time, but I suspect he's a teen. My son, for example, enjoys playing video games or listening to his favorite music

62. Xbox games-music

rappers, men's juicy world, NLE Choppa. Most of the time, my son listens to Lil Uzi Vent and Polo G on YouTube, on his Xbox, or whatever else he listens to. My son would be at school when I went grocery shopping in the morning, or for the majority of the day. In the afternoon, when my son gets off from school, he will go straight to his games and music, and then most of the weekend, Saturday through Sunday, he will be home. My son would be playing on his Xbox and my daughter would be sleeping the majority of the time. When I first walked in with my packages, my son and I were getting ready to put my packages away in the refrigerator and cabinets. The food goes in, but my daughter is graduating from Franklin Senior High School, where I graduated in May 2005 and where I grew up as a teenager. My daughter is 17 and about to turn 18, and my son is 14 and about to turn 15. Sometimes my son would help me with all the packages, so I didn't have to do a thing. anything but a seat until my son has finished putting everything away for me and my

63. packages

teenage daughter wouldn't do anything to help put up the packages. She would be too lazy to do it. I was too tired to put up any of the groceries. My teenage son would do most of the work for me. When I then slaved and did all this walking trying to take care of her and her brother, my daughter doesn't like to clean up after herself at all. We all live together, all three of us. Most of the time, I'll put the groceries away myself. Most of the time, I'll walk all the way to walmart. I would go pick up some things from walmart, like clothes and TVs, and I would call for a taxicab ride from there to come and pick me up because of the heavy TVs I had bought from walmart. I had gotten a 32-inch TV that first day, then I turned around the next day and got a 50-inch TV within that one month to put in my room. I've got two TV screens. First, I bought myself a 32-inch TV when I thought it was too small. Then, I saw the 50-inch TV. I wanted to go back and get it. I would buy a TV, clothes, milk, and food. I would buy it at walmart. I would sometimes need a ride home.

64. taxi cab

I'll call a taxi cab for a ride home. I'll pay the taxi cab $5 to come pick me up from walmart when I feel like I bought too much stuff. I needed a ride home, so sometimes I would buy the smallest items from Walmart and walk back home with them. I have it in my hands and when I walk to the stores or where I need to go, like Family Dollar or Dollar General, I'd walk there for the same small items. I'd walk to get something to eat at Burger King as well. I like Domino's, Subway, Sonic, Forest Restaurant, and McDonald's, but I would never go too far to McDonald's. I'll pass it up for other food restaurants that are nearby, because unless I ever go to McDonald's, I'll go soon, but not at the moment. But whenever I go, I will always have K.O.K wings and things. It would be close to my rented brick home apartment near my home, where I live and absolutely love to eat out nearby. I would walk out of my home to cross the street by the gravesite. That's where I lived, right across the street from the gravesite, to get some private time away from my

65. No worries

two teenage children to go get me something to eat from K.O.K wings and tings. Sometimes I'd buy K.O.K wings and tings for the both of us because that would be the first place I went to besides the subway close by my home to hitch height. I'd be offered a ride, and I'd decline because I don't trust some people who offer me rides. Then I'd go straight home to where I needed to go. No worries, I'm good. Then again, I didn't have enough money to go to any concerts. It was never enough money for me to go anywhere anyway. I'd have to spend it because I'd have to because I needed it or my son needed it. But still, the money was not good enough to say, "Let's enjoy traveling somewhere on a vacation because I couldn't afford it." I was always broke with no money. I had to save up sometimes to get the same different-inch TV when that COVID-19 check came in, but saving didn't work to keep money in my pocket. The bills will always run me down my ass with two

66. allowance

government checks for me, my daughter, and my son child support every week. It would always need to be paid for bills and it could never be saved. My son weekly allowance was needed for clothes and shoes on his back as well as with the fixed income we had. I had no job to turn to. It was hard for me to find one every time I used to fill out an application. I would not get a return call from them because I would fail walmart application tests multiple times trying to get cart attendant and janitorial associate jobs, so I couldn't work. There's no possible way I would see or this could ever happen for me to take a trip to travel anywhere outside the city of Atlanta, GA to see Lil Baby perform at one of his concerts. I am not rich, so this could not happen to me. I see he has a concert in New Orleans at Dave Dixon Dr. Space on October 17th, 2021. I was researching concerts online and came across a Lil Baby concert that was scheduled for that day

67. struggling

Lil Baby performs on the same day as other artists. I've always wanted to see him. on stage, but this could never happen because I would always be busy because my money was funny. It will act strangely, as if I am broke and always struggling. I struggled. I stayed in my local spot in my hometown in Louisiana, which is not going anywhere. If I don't travel, it will still never happen if I do start. Traveling in the future has passed me by plenty of times for me and things have not changed for me. I would think about it as the days passed, but it would never happen for me to go see Lil Baby when things had changed for me. I had struggled for a very long time and I had never been to a concert before in my life. My future was about being broke as the years had flown by for me, wishing, hoping, and praying that when the new future came for me, it would begin a new journey for me. I would start a new future for me to take a turn around to be successful because I know there is a new second chance for my brand new future in the future I want be

68. Jacquees is shabby

broke anymore. now, I'm not all into seeing Jacquees anymore since it's over between me and him. It was just a Facebook thing, nothing serious between us. He said if I didn't act right he was going to leave me. In other words, I left him. Jacquees is shabby and worn out because I was only interested in Lil Baby when I first saw him. I was like, "Oh my Mann!" Dominique Jones is gorgeous. Years ago, while I was having a conversation and flirting with Jacquees, I was having a sexual relationship with Paw, but to make this clear, I am not into women, but I see all this going down. I ain't having it and I am straight. What really drew me to this man, Lil Baby, is his beauty and honesty. With great attention to how in life, Lil Baby makes things work in his rap games so tight that I said, "One day I hope we become soulmates one day in life if Lil Baby lets it happen." Lil Baby was the only man I was really into. I liked that no other man mattered but Lil Baby. I still do, but in a romantic way. He's my man and always will be

69. positive feedback

my number one man for life. I hope we enjoy it. In the future, we will become best friends. I got great positive feedback from one of my psychic readers. I had asked a question about a date. It's a date between me and Lil Baby. I was very happy because I had plans to see him soon. I really like him for one thing, it's a Lil baby thing and my thing about being beautiful black dates that love to get out here and there to explore our careers and push our strengths to get what we want out of life. It's a go-getter situation for us trying to make it as successful as possible. We've been there and done that famous career. No further than that, everything is awesome and as successful as walking out. Bringing the two of us out as single people. My psychic reader was like, "You will date Lil baby." He does look good for you. If he hasn't contacted you, reach out to him. I was happy, really happy, And, yes, I was overjoyed to learn that my Lil baby was going on a date with me to discuss this situation

70. Refresh and pace yourself

to meet him but just wondering how things could be with Lil Baby and me being cool together. It will bring a good closeness between me and Lil Baby and I. I just want to talk to Lil Baby in general. I want to bring us close attention to each other. I just want Lil Baby to know me as a good person. I'm not looking for anything less through these words. Maybe something big will come through these words, because we both don't know each other at this moment and have never seen each other in person to know each other besides this social media. We have seen each other in public research. I believe he did because I already had a book out called "Good-vs-Evil: The Truth Speaker Old School" because I didn't want Jacquees in the first place. Lil Baby is who he truly is. But to get to know Lil Baby as a wonderful man to both me and us, I was looking at Dominique Jones' Instagram and Facebook and I saw that Lil Baby said some shit just gets old! Refresh and pace yourself. You got this! I said the same thing as Lil Baby

71. romance between us

I agree that we need to recharge our batteries in order to move forward in our lives, but with that being said, in order to move forward in our lives, but with that being said, Lil Baby was the answer to what I made of a great romance between us. We will be getting together in the future. My answer to Lil Baby's questions will never go unanswered. Lil Baby status as a rap star makes me curious. I want to know what I should do to get to know him well and not make him my future. But what will happen if we do get to know each other in person, since I've heard he has a huge crush on me? Imma meet him in August 2022? So what is his interest in me? because I was thinking about fun things. If that's so, private is natural, but what else? So will I be financially successful when this happens? Is he going to meet me in Atlanta because I live in Franklin, Louisiana? And I got an answer-back. It looks like he has a huge crush on you, has a good heart and good intentions, and hopes that you and he can get to know each other more and hope something can develop. Yes, you will be financial

72. long-term

enough when this happens, he will want to meet up. I see him coming to see you. So, I was just checking in on me and Lil baby future together to see what's good with us sexually. I find him really fine and I want to get to know him and to not feel some played when I meet him. I'm just hoping things turn out great between us. I'm really digging him. It looks like he feels the same way about you, and he really likes you as well, and I do see things working out for you and him. I see that you and him will be together long term. looks like he's very attracted to you. I had asked to make sure if it wasn't all about sex between me and Lil Baby. I called him by the name Dominique Jones. The psychic said, "This month we are going out on a date." I was like, what? I thought I was on a date when I become successful, and I knew damn well that Lil Baby wasn't coming in to see me in September or October. There was something wrong with that situation. It couldn't be between those months. We had to see each other in the future

73. huge crush

"Lil baby," I said, "Lil baby is coming now." I was like, "I don't think so." I felt it in my spirit that wasn't true, but I knew this thing he had for me was a huge crush, that he liked me and I liked him. I see that it is going to be next month that you and him do go on a date. It looks like it'll go well. Yes, it's going to be there this month or next month that you go on a date. Yes, you will be successful, and I see you enjoying each other's company on this date, and it looks like you will be seeing each other soon. I see that it's going to be currently and not in the future because his feelings are getting stronger for you and he's also going to respond to you and open up to you. My reader probably said it was happening now, not in the future, not saying we went on a date that he liked me now and it was going to happen, but I didn't see this happen for us just yet in September or October 2021 or I haven't become successful just yet within those two months! And I was like, "Wait, how does he know me by looking me up in Google search about my book.

74. Lil Baby-Paw

Because it's everywhere on social media and on Facebook, Lil Baby must've researched for my first book, Good-Vs-Evil. I have never talked to him before or met him before, and how is he going to reach me through Twitter, Instagram, or Facebook because I didn't know he knew me and my Good-Vs-Evil book? "Yes, he knows," my reader said, and I agreed. Yes, he did look for my book. He also saw it on social media. Yes, even though you and him never talked, he's going to reach out to you through social media. You don't know him personally, but it looks like he wants to get to know you. Yea, Lil baby wants to get to know me. Yea, yea, my friend, paw right yea, but I see it looks like this friend of yours does like you. Yea, it's me. Paw likes me. I've been dating my long-term partner for some time now, and I see that he has feelings for you and he is soon going to want to be in a relationship with you. My reader was talking about me and my man-paw.

75. chocolate pink pussy

Sorry, family or people, but Paw should have brought me around to his family and friends way before his ex came back into the picture. They were nowhere in the picture when we were together. I can't do that. There's no way it could possibly happen to us. I was hurt twice by paw. I am not doing this at all with him. I have a successful plan to write a book now about me and this pink pussy flower of mine, since this chocolate pink pussy in the middle makes this man go crazy, so I don't have to repeat it and how much I bathe to keep this pussy clean of mine. I have to take care of myself. It's going to be called "Pink Pussy Flower"—a gift It's how he acts the title and subtitle, and I am so grateful for life. Praise the heavenly father. But though I'm looking to win in life, because it would be better in life to stand out and watch things flow with myself as a single person, a woman I am, But can you believe it? Lil Baby made that humble rap happen, but can you believe it? I jammed to Lil Baby song. But I was hitting that shit hard when I first heard how humble it was

76. greatest hits

Poppin For one thing, please believe it was one of my favorite greatest hits ever. I am telling you, it was one of my favorite greatest hits of all time. Please believe me boo. I would never consider listening to any other type of music. Nobody does the humble better than Lil Baby kk. I posted one of his pictures in all white with a hat on my facebook page. Everything was white, so everything that fit, Lil Baby had on at his concert. I used the hashtag #LilBabyAndFriends to tag Lil Baby and his pals. I was talking about it. "Lil Baby was going to be that age when he turned 27 in December 2021." Every time I would see a Dreez video, I would be like, "It really stands out excellent with a Dreez white T-shirt and yellow pants." "Doing her beatbox dance was great, though I saw Dreez wore white shoes." I am so excited to see Dreez make that move on her birthday with her mom." Serena Romero was doing her beatbox dance in the Dreez video. I got up after 11:30 AM on Friday, May 7, at night time just

77. gorgeous

because I was sleeping all day, I had to get myself some rest after all the typing I was doing about me and Dreez on how beautiful and gorgeous we are as lady sisters, and Dreez is looking so fly with her dress code and makeup on, but to me, Dreez doesn't need any makeup on her face because Dreez is so beautiful without makeup on. Sis, you get it with those giddy girls' daisy dukes on sweet honey chocolate sis, but like I was saying, I got up around 11:30 PM on May 7, Friday to grab some milk and ginger snaps that I bought from the Franklin supermarket in my home town of Franklin, LA, but I'ma get to that part later because it's after 12 AM on my time. On Saturday, May 8, 2021, at 12:23 a.m. on my phone, I looked at the time to see what time it was. It was Mother's Day. Yes, I am a mother. Happy Mother's Day to me and Mother's Day is tomorrow. I'm going to drink some E & J PEACH brandy with natural peach flavors with the caramel color, but as I said on Saturday, May the 7th, Friday, I'm going to grab me

78. purchased

some of my favorite milk since I am a milk drinker. I love to drink low-fat milk. 1% milk fat, 1 GAL (3.78L) purple label with a green circle saying "add flavor to life food club," a blue circle saying "8g protein per serving," and a white circle saying "But this time I had to pay cash for all four gallons of milk, so the four boxes of cereal cost me $95 at Franklin supermarket." I could name them right now, it's the morning after 12:41 AM. The time keeps changing since it's still Saturday, May 8, 2021. Since I'm up so late in bed typing, I should just name all the cereals I bought. Since I lost my food stamps, I purchased $95 worth of groceries with my cash. Corn pops are sweet. The Frosted Flakes cereals from Kellogg's are GR-R-REAT!'s, apple & cinnamon jacks sweetened cereal, cinnamon toast, and General Mills Kellogg's. I had to reapply.

79. BIG 50" TV

Eating my snacks I woke up to eat late at night. I started to put that Dreez Bday beatbox song on my Roku BIG 50" TV. I finally have cable now and can watch whatever I want. I was struggling to get cable in my home to watch TV, but now I have to train myself to watch TV again. I have that wireless connection with cox communication for $40 per month to watch my cable. It's free to watch Roku on my BIG 50" TV. One day I was watching Dreez on my big screen TV on YOUTUBE and it was my favorite song, Bday Beatbox with Dreez and Dreez Mom, Serena Romero and Dreez Mom. Both were big as cuffs on my screen TV. I watched both of them. The video made my day. The bad thing about it is that my two old big flat-screen TVs went on. I'm glad to gain back two flat-screen TVs, but can I believe I'm up at 2:11 in the morning typing trying to make this dream bread happen for me? Oh yea, I'm going to get this. I'm going to make it happen even if I have to give a push and a shove too

80. cherish

make anything happen for me. I'm going to do this, so whatever my heavenly father referred me to, I'm going to do it because I don't want to make anything out of something I can cherish myself for eternal life, which is book publishing, so I'm sending all my books to Balboa Press and wishing and hoping. I'm hoping for a book signing with my name, Anastacia Burrell, to be in the works. Sure, it will happen to me. I know it will. I'll be right there with my sister. with this success in the future. Dreezy, when I get everything organized, Balboa Press will be the place where I'll be publishing with them for now and forever. Let's make my career an achievement to win in my life. I won, as I said, so I will make that a proper win to make things happen for me. I got it, so I deserve more than life can bring to me. I have a successful career and am a stay-at-home mother of two teenage children, a son and a daughter. I work hard. My efforts paid off with the good work I worked for. If I work hard enough to get it with my hard work, nobody else will.

81. deserve

I deserve a fancy home from my hard work as a writer. I pray to be patient with hard work. I love what I do as an author. My books are published at home on my laptop. I do my own thing all day on my laptop every chance I get. So I'm going to do it. I need to get it to see how I live and lead my life because I am not a follower, I am a leader. That's why I will take life as it goes for me because I have the power to do so. So it doesn't matter what the situation is. Maybe I got this because I play the game raw in my everyday life. There ain't nobody blocking me out of my blessings unless I block myself out of the game of life's success. I want to go and get my sister so I can hold her down like me. I can go get it myself. Nobody is bigger than me. Try me. My eyes do not hurt for people. I am not afraid. The devil is a lie. I got the power I am not a weak woman. I know my spirit and my heavenly father knows me well spiritually in my soul. I would never take life for granted because it is too easy because hard work would get me there with plenty of

82. carrier

efforts and it's not going to give me a return on my effort to keep money in my pocket and not to spend my money on someone that's not worth spending it on because it's not theirs for me to spend on. I'm just the carrier, not a provider. And speaking of me being a star, it's most likely my sister Dreez making her rap game cool too. The world makes plenty of fans like me too. The author is to write that I am to turn my books into movies. I'm going to do this by the bundle. I'm serious about making money flow into my life. I can do this. Watch me flow, because I can do whatever it takes to make my efforts happen for me to live a happy ever after as a strong woman. I am worth it. I am a superwoman doing superwoman things. It doesn't hurt to find or pick a piece of paper up with an ink pin or type and start telling the world exactly what's on in my mind on a written piece of paper or type exactly what's on my mind into the laptop. I open my laptop every single time to professional thoughts. I can do this on every try and every chance

83. Disney World

I have to get to a level of thinking about something and have to give it a try. What I do is real. I do this too. I think about getting out of life too. I dream big about traveling and doing other things with my life. When is it starting for me? Well, I have to think about this beginning to start a new career. It'll take me far enough to travel in life too. Saving money to go straight to Disney World is the only way to make my dreams of living the life I want come true. I have to get it and some more, but the thing is that looking ahead will be better for me to be a better person. author/book writer out of me. My life is just a phone call away. It won't be too far to get it either. Trust and believe I've got bigger and better things to do with my life. What motivates me and Dreez to travel the world and party nonstop with me? One of these days, my sister and I will rock the house with a few drinks and set up a jam music party in Atlanta, Georgia. I see Dreez there all the time in one of those hotel rooms because Dreez is set, Dreez

84. pool hall

can get any hotel she wants. I saw Dreez playing at a pool hall. I saw a pool hall where Dreez was. In one of the Dreez videos, she had a close-up with a pool hall in her hand. Another thing I saw was Dreez sitting on a white cover and blanket in a mirror. Dreez was on her phone taking pictures. I bet Dreez was on a ball, having the best time of her life. I wished to meet Dreez while having an enjoyable alone time. I believe Dreez was by herself, quality time by herself. I saw Dreez alone in the room, but I know Dreez doesn't ever be alone because I always see Dreezy with someone or somebody and her mom, Serena Romero, but truly I did see Dreez by herself. Sometimes it is good for her to be alone by herself, because sometimes it is good for me to have some alone time by myself. I love to have quality alone time to myself and I would like to fit into the ATL, GA groove sometime soon when I get there. I have never been to Atlanta or California. That's where Dreez's hometown is, but Dreez is originally from California, a beautiful city.

85. I am country-creole

Symbolically, we are very different. Besides, I am a country-creole Louisiana girl, and Dreez is a city girl from California. So I'm making it happen where I live, and Dreez is already on the ball like I am. I've got this all day, every damn day. I want to make big bucks, so I will, me and myself, and I. That's all I got. That's what I found out in the end. Talking about partying, that's one thing I'm going to do: party and celebrate in the future. I saw Dreez partying on Instagram all the time, and her other sisters were out at nightclubs, but Imma made it happen one day. There may be no lose or fail situations, no do or die situations, it's all return, so Imma live life well and enjoy being a prophetess. I will drink wine because of the joy of happiness. Yes, heavenly Father, I will be happy for all the kingdoms I live for, but aside from that, I will make everything big in my life. This is going to be very real for me. I will make an epic out of it. Please believe me when I say I will trust my words. I can do this.

86. hometown

there was never a high mountain. I couldn't do this at all, but it's the life of me and everything I will do and go out and do things. I am not a party pooper, but I am damn sure if I sit around the house... I like to party by myself most of the time. I like to party by myself all of the time, so I am so alone. Sometimes I am a solo dolo girl, walking around all over places, getting myself something to eat, going to the stores, walking all day long in my hometown in Louisiana. I hustle. I love LA, baby. I ain't going nowhere and I ain't moving out of it. I am here to stay, but the only thing is, I may travel. Don't get me wrong, maybe sometimes. Then come back home to Louisiana. ATL is OK, though, but not to stay. I will never live in Atlanta. I'll go out there and stay for a couple of days. I don't have family out there anyway, so I'll be out there by myself in the hotel having a good time drinking by myself, but there's no telling what I might get myself into. I'm going to find myself happy one of these days, and nobody can take it from me or destroy it. Yup, that is it! I'm going to be so shocked

87. faithfully

awoke in a cheerful mood. I am not going to know how to stop or act while living a good life that I will achieve faithfully. It's all done, it will get done. Right now I'm sipping on some sonic drink with ice, which is orange juice "honey". I got the orange juice fever and, plus, I'm laying in bed just chilling. I'm trying to find something to do, but at home, all I can do is chill and think about what a good life is coming for me and me alone, not anybody else but myself. So I'ma break this off one more time and again! Lawdddd It's nighttime, just not my day trying to think of something to talk about, but though I do indeed have it on my mind, seriously, when I do it will come out, it's after 12:13 AM on Sunday, May 16 at night. I am still up, wishing this time would fly by for me. I am hoping something will make a change for the better for me. Yea, I've been up at night lately straight-forward on my laptop just thinking about something to do for efforts to make seed to shower for me to make it in life to see where my goals are headed and dreams. Just thinking about

88. hopefully

my plans include the following: I have to make it in life. I know that's right. For me, just getting out of bed, I don't have any food in the refrigerator. The ups and downs are real. I'll be damned if I go any longer without food stamps. I had to reapply again. I've just filed. I submitted my application as soon as I received my mail in my mailbox yesterday, Saturday, May 15th, afternoon sunrise, in order to get my food stamp back again. I have to get that done. Hopefully, the food stamp office people won't stop it again. I'm just ready to get my food stamp back again. I need some food in my house. I just got hungry earlier today when I went to take that walk in the daytime. I went to get myself a sonic cheese combo burger to eat because I was hungry as hell. I had to eat and all that walking had me tired and my back hurting for one thing. I was taking meds for back pain, but it seems like my back still aches and I could use some spa treatment to help with this back aching pain I have every now and then. I see that Dreez sis has

89. yummy yummy

it going on cooking in her videos, but I can't remember everything Dreez cooks, but I know Dreez be cooking. All I could see was meatloaf. Yum, yum, yum. I got that yummy yummy "LOL" and some other soul food cooking Dreez was doing. I believe Dreez had a top chief in some way. Dreez was also the top chef, cooking in the kitchen occasionally. It looked delicious so far. I noticed the girl in the kitchen cooking. I noticed that we both enjoy fried chicken. One of my favorite meals is fried chicken, but I also enjoy honey and hot sauce on my fried chicken. I didn't get to taste the sauce. Dreezy said, "I saw Dreez eat that chicken in that video and it was greasy and perfect." I'm about to be the top chef in the kitchen pretty soon. I can cook too now. I try, "Oh yesss, baby." I can throw it down in the kitchen. I can whip up something great. Yes dear, I can cook soul food and country cooking. Louisiana I was born and raised in Louisiana and I can't believe I haven't gone to the city part of New Orleans yet but

90. goals

soon, when I reach the base of this dream, I will have fully achieved my goals to the best of my ability. I'ma be a successful writer. Imma get-there boo all the way, 100% and tasting this honey and hot sauce are amazing. I can't get enough of pouring honey with hot sauce on my chicken. In the kitchen, that's my favorite root flavor. Well, well, it's been after so much, so I've been up all night doing nothing but watching TV. Yup, that's all I can do right now is live my normal life in bed while cooling. This single life is fun. I enjoy every moment of it. thank god for this. I'm never getting married to Paw. I don't have time for a grown man that stays on top of me looking for money and effort to put in his pocket. Though I should know who that may be, Paw actions speak louder than words. Yup, I don't have time for games. I am a woman that needs to be loved and needs affection. I also need attention. I know Dreez understands what I am talking about. For one thing, my sister understands that I do not need a man to get another woman pregnant on me. This has happened more than once

91. enough said

but there is no telling when this might happen to me again. I never know what paw is up to. The bad paw is always surprising me with down shit, but Star has the nerve to say paw made babies on me, but no bitch paw didn't make babies on me and paw played shonta for so many years, plenty of times for me shaking my head. I guess shonta was married to Paw for longer than I was, but I don't think so. I was with paw when shonta wasn't, but enough said about this shonta shit. It's about Dreez and me, my sister girl, but we will always do it for the fame, right Dreez. WOW! I think I need to get some sleep. It's 3:17 a.m. on Sunday, May 16, 2021. There is so much toxic in my life in a relationship with a man who wants to cheat on me these days. Paw! Yea, that's him. I don't get enough credit for it. What paw does behind my back, I can do better with or without paw. I am doing excellent without my paw. This new year is passing by so fast that I can't even stand a chance of getting by this new year, and before I know it, another new year will be coming in

92. club at a young age

soon and then when another new year comes to pass, that's going to go in fast to lawdddd, I am so tired right now that I can just go to sleep while I am lying in my bed. Well, I'm already in bed, so I'm going to take a rest myself for the night and go to sleep here. I need some sleep to get up in the morning. Now it's 4:10 PM in the evening in the daytime and I've been wanting to get up in the morning. But though I stayed in bed all morning until it was time for me to get up and out of bed, instead, I got on my snapchat to speak about how I snuck into the club at a young age. When I was eighteen years old growing up as a teenager, it was at Joe's lounge in my hometown. The first time I went in, that's the only club I remember going to besides other clubs downtown and that other club in Centerville Louisiana only accepts those under the age of 24 into that club. I went to clubs in Louisiana over the years since I have been living in Saint Mary Parish for a very long time. I went to J.A. Hernandez Elementary School, LaGrange Elementary, and Franklin Junior High

93. graduated

School, Franklin Senior High School I graduated with all my classmates at the end of the 12th-grade year in 2005 from Franklin Senior High School. I was a student and a classmate at "05" High School Graduate. I love my hometown in Louisiana. I hate the city. I am not a city girl. For one thing, I could never live in the city. For another, it's great to travel from place to place. Like I was saying, I will. I love to travel but not to live in the city. My dream would be to go to Disney World to go out and have fun on a vacation by myself, maybe to get away for a moment to get away from everybody, because sometimes I need some time alone and space to breathe and focus on myself first and to maintain what my life is all about: getting away and taking life as it goes. Not too long ago, I just finished eating some spaghetti that mom had brought leftovers to my house to eat with some hot sauce. Now I want a pepperoni personal pan pizza to eat, so I'm thinking about going to subway and getting myself a personal pizza in a box. I was wondering what time it was so I could go to the subway

94. pretty tasty

and order me some pizza to eat. As a matter of fact, I'm going to get myself something to eat right now, which is pizza. Who's a pizza lover, meee? Who doesn't love pizza? and some soda pop to go with my pizza. I'm thirsty again. This religious woman needs some pizza. I'm going to get myself some pizza. I was thinking about some E & J for sho' though. That subway is an extra white cheese pizza with jalapeno peppers and big pepperoni. It's so good in the hot subway white box with the green and yellow words written on top of the box, and some of the two chocolate chip cookies were OK. The subway chocolate chip cookies were pretty tasty. The subway cookies are alright. I like my chocolate chip cookies with milk instead of soda pop to drink with them, and I had an orange fanta soda with my pizza that I bought from subway and with my white plastic handbag that I got from subway restaurant as well. I walked out of my brick apartment to go get some subway pizza! I live right at the back of subway Road, so I

95. typical daily

took a chance and went for a walk to get something from the subway. I enjoyed the walk all the way to the subway and back home, and then I went into my room to sit down and relax after a long day of walking. I went to get some dinner pizza for supper this evening, so I'm going to get a meal today. Wow, time is passing by so quickly. I don't want to say fast, it's just moving like I haven't been to sleep long enough in this pandemic un-normal. It's like I go to sleep the next day and I get the feeling that time is passing on my laying time of sleep. It's the time, the time. Something is wrong with me getting up and around. Time is really flying by, it's not like a normal sleep, an abnormal, typical daily day, and I'm like, what's wrong with me sleeping and waking up? I'm starting to not like this time. I really like nighttime more than I like getting up in the morning and afternoon after 12 PM. Today is Monday, May 17. I have to get up and go somewhere. I have to go and come back later. I'm on my grind again. I've got to hustle by

96. pandemic

myself without any support from my family or side man paw, I'm not looking for support either. With that said, I have to fax my food stamp papers to the family stamp office to get some packages into this home of mine. I'm renting from the landlord, so I'm grinding and trying to get mine back soon. Guess what? I thought it was after 12 PM, so I had to look at my time just to see what time it was. It was after 12:53 AM in the morning. I thought I had to get back on my grind in the afternoon. "LOL," I thought I had a good sleep, which I did. I'm still in bed from yesterday great pizza, in which I had extra white cheese, jalapeno peppers, and large pepperonis. But, as I previously stated, the pandemic of the abnormal is spreading like wildfire from country to country, particularly in my home state of Louisiana. I didn't think it was in the afternoon, but I had then slept the day away. That's why I thought I had to get up in the afternoon to hustle to take care of my business at the food stamp office.

97. local office

The local office will make the fax to the food stamp office in New Iberia because that's where the local office is located with the food stamp office people and everything, so I was in bed at 2:02 AM Monday morning, January 17th, the day to go fax my food stamp papers. I thought it was time for me to get up to do what I had to do, but really, though time does pass by weary, I had a lack of sleep. That's all. It wasn't a mistake. Right now, I am on my cell phone looking things up. I just love being on the internet to see what's positive going on. I need to know I can work with my goals for the future for myself, so I'ma put a price tag on that. Though I can't wait to get up this morning to fax my papers to the family office, I have to get up and do everything I can do to push hard in life and plus brush my teeths to start my beautiful day off right. I've got to get up out of bed and off the internet. I search for too many things to get by that are positive. So I'm a big dreamer. It's nothing I wouldn't do to sit around and do nothing because I'm going to find something to do and I am laying underneath my

98. prayers

fan with the cold air breeze as I wait for the sun to rise and shine for me to be happy with myself first. And God in heaven will always come first in my worship. I just love being in the Lord's house. I am being good to myself and my heavenly father up above. Yes, I do and preach the word of God in the bible verses, the holy spirit of goodness. I am spiritually in Christ's word and have white sages. My first plan would be to pray to God in heaven for what I want out of life and hope that god hears my prayers. Every second and every moment and every hour, God hears my prayers up above. I LOVE GOD with a passion. My father is my father, a father, a father. AMEN I know times get hard, but praise God and omen! And as for the father up above, I will seek this day forward in the father God. He is a person. He is the son of God. He is God, and man is the devil. I am a child of God up above. I'm not a devil worshiper, but though it looks like I'm going to pull an all-nighter here, I believe it's just a chance to get off of social media. I'm just letting this time pass me by. Not in front of me though

99. patience

because I'm in the front, not in the back, so I can get by this morning because I'm still up. Monday, May 17, 3:24 a.m., and as I type on my cell phone, I will make this day go by smoothly with patience. I will go get it and make myself proud of everything I do. Falling asleep underneath this fan is worth it. I'm feeling so sleepy. I can't go to sleep right now because I'm still up doing what I need to do laying across my bed with the fan on top of my head. I'm cold with the cover on top of my head. When I do get up to brush my teeth, like I already said, I will do that. That's what I'ma do because I need to get everything straight. I have to keep moving around to get somewhere to make it. I'm trying to have everything organized in my life by doing things by myself. That's what I have to do to have everything organized in the morning so I can get up to brush my teeth. That's the most important thing: getting up and moving around, seeing things, trying to have things work for buying and trying to have things are

100. sister dreez

not free, especially having the government close my case with my food stamps. I have to stay on top of that to have groceries in my home to survive. If I said my food stamp case worker had cut me off, it's still the same thing as closing my case. I want my food stamps back after this morning. I can't wait until they open for me to fax those papers. I was wondering what my sister Dreez was up to because I saw her cutting up with that old girl dumping her booty from the back at the club. I didn't know who she was. It seems to me that she didn't look familiar to me. The girl, Dreezy, was dumping her booty from the back. I've seen her in the company of successful celebrities too, dreez. I saw Dreez with a white woman with a cream-yellow mini skirt on, and Dreez had a shiny leather burgundy top on and some black shiny leather jeans on. What I saw in the club with that video on Instagram and back to this pandemic virus spreading all over, I want my own TV show like Tiffany Pollard. She had her own television show with celebrities, taking taxi cabs to restaurants, Tiffany Meets Celebrities.

* 9 7 8 9 3 5 6 1 0 7 1 4 4 *